I ASK MY SISTER'S GHOST

✺

I ASK MY SISTER'S GHOST

✽

BENJAMIN GUCCIARDI

NEW MICHIGAN PRESS
TUCSON, ARIZONA

NEW MICHIGAN PRESS
DEPT OF ENGLISH, P. O. BOX 210067
UNIVERSITY OF ARIZONA
TUCSON, AZ 85721-0067

<http://newmichiganpress.com>

Orders and queries to <nmp@thediagram.com>.

Copyright © 2020 by Benjamin Gucciardi.
All rights reserved.

ISBN 978-1-934832-73-8. FIRST PRINTING.

Design by Ander Monson.

Cover image courtesy of the author.

CONTENTS

Advice for Pallbearers   1
I Ask My Sister's Ghost How Dying Is   3
The Hermitage at Laurel Dell   5
I Ask My Sister's Ghost How Her Days Are Now   7
About the Election, the Poet Answered   9
Prayer for the Instant City   10
Spill   14
I Ask My Sister's Ghost to Play a Game of Cribbage   16
Looking for Chanterelles in the Oakland Hills   18
The Arachnologist   20
I Ask My Sister's Ghost to Take Me with Her   22
Masa   24
Rendering the Pose   26
Chosen Landscape   45

Acknowledgments   49

Ideal and dearly beloved voices
of those who are dead, or of those
who are lost to us like the dead.

Sometimes they speak to us in our dreams;
sometimes in thought the mind hears them.

And for a moment with their echo other echoes
return from the first poetry of our lives—
like music that extinguishes the far-off night.

—C.P. Cavafy

ADVICE FOR PALLBEARERS

To make the sound
of your footsteps disappear

requires practice,
a cornfield in late autumn

when the ground is brittle enough
to repeat what it hears.

Best if the six of you can go together
at dusk, find a barn-owl,

a corn-crow will do.
See how close you can get

before the bird startles, observe
the interaction of air and wing.

Before you handle the casket,
borrow your mother's finest crystal

vase, carry it through the crowded parking lot
to the water park, ride the slides.

Let nothing shatter.
The trick is for the coffin to appear

to float, the weight of his failures
superfluous. Let him be known

as a saint, for a few moments,
before he takes up haunting.

I ASK MY SISTER'S GHOST HOW DYING IS

And she weighs the oath of secrecy the dead take
against the pact we made in the crawl space

beneath the front porch, our birthmarks
pressed together, her cheek against my wrist.

She looks over both shoulders,
leans in—it's like gathering dolls from the debris

of the great Pacific plastic patch,
filling your dinghy with their pale figures,

lying down among them the way we hid
in tupelo. Like one doll taking your hand

and you realize she's lost two fingers
as the boat drifts beyond the plastic

and the stars begin to boil
in the navy sky. Like knowing the story

of every constellation is wrong,
trying to tell the dolls

Orion is a butterfly mistaken for a warrior
when they begin to sing the Magnificat

in chorus, place a thousand hands
on your body, tug your eyelids into position.

Two by two they turn, making no splash
as they leave you to your laughter,

mixing with the brine. Her voice quiets.
I realize my eyes are closed

when I open them and find myself
alone in dim light beneath my father's porch,

the wind slipping through slats,
something scratching in the corner.

THE HERMITAGE AT LAUREL DELL

Of a life playing Bach for moss
on a swollen cello,

lying for days
in a field of milkmaids,

undressing in fog to translate Jeffers—
wolle, entfernung, stein, Wahrheit,

only six rotted railroad ties remain
and a few microfiche slides

of Emil Barth's meticulous cursive
filling the page—*A buck,*

plus what's foraged, feeds you well enough,
he wrote in his journal,

March eight, nineteen sixteen,
but a boar, salted and cured, is divine.

When the poets came to visit,
he didn't tell them he was unhappy,

nearly always sick.
He toasted with plum mead,

laughed at stories of their trysts.
So what, touch haunts you,

he told himself when they'd gone,
drinking from the spring,

scrubbing his doubt with clear water,
the bombs would fall, anyway.

I ASK MY SISTER'S GHOST HOW HER DAYS ARE NOW

Do you remember those picture books
where the illustrator removes the outer wall

of a jumbo jet to show children where luggage goes,
how the pilots' levers connect to wings?

Where cross-section diagrams reveal
the way smoke escapes through stacks

in a sugar factory, the four hundred yellow-tipped
missiles a warship's hull can hold?

And how in some diagrams
you could find a bathroom in the schema,

and a nail-sized man with blue pants around his ankles
reading the paper while quietly shitting?

I feel just like that man now.
Doing my business, everyone oblivious

to my presence, and if by chance they see me,
they chuckle, as if my lone role is to make light

of the pain on the pilot's face,
the underpaid laborers threshing cane,

the marines playing ping-pong
as the turrets open

and we rain down hellfire on the next village
where the word for *beauty*

sounds just like the word for *camel*, and the phrase
I borrowed sometimes means *I burned.*

ABOUT THE ELECTION, THE POET ANSWERED

    even after

his comrades

    were slaughtered,

his brother disappeared,

    people mostly

asked him to read

    the love sonnets

he'd written

    in his twenties.

PRAYER FOR

In the makeshift mosque, twenty-four men kneel,
heads pressed to the straw carpet.
In white linen, khaki slacks,
they bend like egrets in the shallows,
stalking God's love,
that sweet, rasping toad.

Beside their fathers,
the smallest boys pray.
I have never seen my father bow
but once in the woods
after my sister's death
he called the ground up to him.
Eyes closed, leaning into filtered light,
the leaves and the soil
came, the ants crawled
across his prayer.

THE INSTANT CITY

Look at the marks on their foreheads,
Hasan tells me, as we begin
our shift. *You can see who prays the most.*
We are delivering tents
for the hundreds that arrive
from Homs, Aleppo,
the villages between.
A camp becomes a city
the way a wound
becomes a scar.

When we were children,
my sister buried my father
to the neck in coarse sand.
He smiled as her yellow pail
emptied on his chest.
I placed a chipped
white limpet over each
of his eyes.

The Arabic script tilts, each hymn
a calligraphy of ships
the imam steers,
his voice like water
slapping the hull, a call
plaited voices answer—
by You we enter the evening,
by You we enter the morning.
The ship's wake widens
into silence.

SPILL

I follow my father down a corridor
of laurel. Where I see wild,
he sees symmetry—
red trillium
refutes winter's theorem,
distant ridges divide place
into watershed,
basin.

I don't understand this mathematics
he makes of the world,
but I follow close
in case he speaks,
tasting yarrow, sorrel,
when he picks it.

The trail opens at the tainted river.
When the samples are capped,
levels tallied in a ledger
no one will see,
he rolls up the sleeve of my sweater.

His finger traces the path
of the spill's damage,
or is he reading my palm?
Naming the crease
where the heart-line fuses
with the head.

I know not to ask what might come.
Cup my hand
as if guarding a damselfly.

I ASK MY SISTER'S GHOST TO PLAY A GAME OF CRIBBAGE

I set up the good board with the mahogany pegs,
warm the bourbon and stir in cider.

We sit between woven peacocks on the Persian rug,
the cards blur and plume as I shuffle them.

You want to know about sex in the afterlife?
We never spoke of the body, or its pleasures,

and I don't want to speak of them now.
It's better than poetry, she tells me anyway,

but worse than cheap whiskey.
Better than addiction, but worse than denial.

She completes the crib and we begin the count.
In a peacock's beak, a sprig of wheat shakes in braided wind.

Better than a royal flush, she smiles, laying her cards between us,
but nothing like shooting the moon.

As she moves her pegs up the board I can't help picturing the
    mechanics
of making love without the body—

maybe the slow deliverance of shadows fusing in a field
at dusk. Or perhaps it's more abstract—

a pair of red squares in a white plane, the straight lines breaking,
lacing into eights, settling into a single, momentary sphere.

It's true there are times I've merged without touching.
When I lie down in the meadow where we spread your ashes,

it's as if the earth seeps into me, unfurls a vine
around my throat. She lowers her cards, picks at the carpet's warp.

Well, she asks, do you like it? And though the grip
nearly splits me, I realize, for the first time, that I do.

LOOKING FOR CHANTERELLES IN THE OAKLAND HILLS

It is not only trauma which cleaves.
The soul also fractures in joy.

All month I summon the shard of myself
still kneeling in the sword-fern,

tracing the forked ridges of winter's first chanterelle,
but it won't leave the scent—

soil pinched with pepper, apricot,
to return to the city,

where another piece of me mutters
under the overpass, looking for a fix.

Sometimes when I plead
for my fragments to join,

I hear my mother's voice,
calling her dead daughter home.

Slow down, my friend insists,
off-trail, in deep woods,

they're easy to miss.
Rain spills from my cap

as I scour the chaparral,
bending to buckeye roots,

digging through duff. *There,*
flesh worthy of the name, *chanterelle.*

I remove the veil of mud
as if it were lace,

I splinter when my fingers slip
the stem from loam.

THE ARACHNOLOGIST

Martel Jenkins was the only black kid in the barrio
who spoke Spanish, and the only friend besides Jesús Cristo
the drunk on the corner called by name.

When he would tell me his teeth felt too heavy
to study history, I excused him.
I knew he was headed for the aqueduct,

or the boarded-up houses choked
by trumpet vine where he found them.
He collected spiders with the discipline of a surgeon.

He kept them in empty soda bottles
under his bed. On his way into sixth period,
he touched my fist with his fist,

announced the genus of his catch,
Latrodectus, and his total, *that's nine this week!*
Through this tally of arachnids captured

in sugary plastic, we learned to trust each other
the way men on tankers far out at sea
confide reluctantly in gray rippling water.

When his best friend broke the news,
they found Martel last night, her voice quavering,
stray bullet off International,

I went to his house to adopt a widowed spider.
I imagined the red hourglass
on the female's abdomen emptying itself

slowly, her segmented body imprisoned
in the glow of the green-tinted bottle,
but no one was home. Now when I hear

the old women gathering cans at dawn,
their bodies half-swallowed by blue waste bins,
I think of Martel finding containers

to bring to the canyon, Martel
inspecting stones, placing his fingers
delicately around the thorax,

the eight legs angry at the morning
as he lifts the arrowhead orb weaver
towards the sun, offering

what he loved to the old, hungry light.

I ASK MY SISTER'S GHOST TO TAKE ME WITH HER

Not because the reefs are bleaching.
Because I want to see how thin the veil is.

To row behind her in the boat
she came in, row all day

into night and where the river turns
to delta, blade my oar to beach the dinghy

on a bank of silt and cattail.
Because I want to hide with her

in midnight's swaying, turn my ears
from the throng of bullfrogs

to the harp song she hums,
listen to her stories of its blind composer,

how he charmed wives at the Royal parties
in Dublin, his fingers sweeping

each glissando, his eyes clouded over
like a cod on ice, waiting to be salted.

Because I want to watch a new sun stain
the sky with colors I've never seen,

swaths I can only hint at with words—
serpentine, tourmaline, silver.

There is a Chinese symbol she taught me for a word
that has no word, but I can never remember

how to draw it, what tone
to put in my throat when I speak it.

The inked shape of that mutable mark hangs
just beyond the last branch of my mind

as she turns to leave.
There is nothing I can say

to convince her to take me,
so I pluck the tongue from my mouth

and lay it flat on a stone.
When she bends to inspect

the petal, it becomes a red door.
It creaks as she opens it,

walks into the unspoken
without turning back.

MASA

I thought my sister's ashes
would feel like masa.
Clumpy, maybe, but milled
free from her figure.

But when I cup a handful
to sow in the canyon
where we gathered nasturtiums,
I greet flame's laziness—

two triangles of bone
intact among the powder—
a vertebrae's corner?
Her middle phalanx

that steadied the blade
she pulled across her wrist?
Arrowheads
we should have left

in the cornfield, cobalt
glass the sea spit up,
or the sails of the toy ship
we captained in the tub,

water sloshing over the porcelain rim
as we summoned a squall
through which only fools
like us would sail.

RENDERING THE POSE

Perspective

I.

After sketching figures, a student rolls up the leg of his jeans
and recounts the accident—Guatemala, the mountain road
where two buses collided in a flash of yellow fury.
My rodilla was aquí, he said, pointing left,
pero my foot was ahí, pointing right, *dangling*.

I picture the buckled buses, cracked windshields
declaring the names of the drivers' lovers
in bright, beveled letters—Lupita, Esmeralda,
one of whom became a widow as traffic backed up
and people left their idling cars
to watch the injured file out carrying the dead.

I'm not sure how he learned that word,
dangling, before the word knee,
but I admire that he used it just the same.
Don't worry mister, he said, turning to leave,
we die seven times before to stop breathing.

II.

If death comes seven times, then my first death
was in realizing the smallness of my life.
That my students' blemished faces
are the only ones my life will touch.
That my paintings will gather in basements,
bargain aisles. That the scent of eucalyptus
drifting through the window in August
will form the strongest memory of this city,
the only city I will call home and mean it.

A strange kind of death, that first dying—
I look toward the vastness of the landscape.
The sea walking always away from the horizon.

III.

Last week, during a self-portrait exercise,
the student drew himself as a fish snared on a hook.
How spare his marks on the page—
the single inked stroke of the pole,
arc of the fishing line, sharp curve of the barb piercing
the fish's mouth, the seething scrawls
implying the surface of water.
Who is the fisherman here? I asked,
his eyes settled on his hands.

IV.

Naming pain is a kind of violence.
A terrible art best done with gesture, allegory.
So that when I say *time hunts with its baited hook*,
I should flash my hand like a lure, for effect.

Or when I say *all day in the eucalyptus grove
I confess myself to starlings*, I mean my human heart
is starving for forgiveness.

And when I answer the phone
and that student stammers on the line,
My uncle locked the door again, he won't let me in,
and I reply, *I'll pick you up, be ready in an hour*—

what I want to say is, *there is a tradition in pottery
where shards are melted down, then pounded again,
to form a stronger clay.*

I want to say, *can I show you the picture I drew of myself
when I was your age? It was like yours. In pencil,
I made myself a spider hanging from thread,
my eight legs flailing.*
Another of my seven deaths.

Weight of the Line

v.

I scoured my room to find the drawing.
In a shoebox full of cowries, slap bracelets, warped pastels—
the last photograph of my family together.
My mother in her favorite dress, my naked body
against the blue linen. My sister, five years old,
stroking my hair, singing as my mother hummed—
I forget the words but not the tune,
not the scent of buckwheat boiling on the stove,
my father's beard like kelp when he kissed us
into barnacle dreams. Not the rhythm
of my mother's rocking. The map she traced on my back—
her fingers circling my birthmark, that dark sun
setting in the lake of my body.
How wholly they believed their love was a cloister.

VI.

At last I found the drawing, the lines faded,
the image now the mark a rock makes
when hurled through a window.
I considered how to explain this to the student:
The window is the holy family, I am the rock, we all need rebellion.
Or maybe, *I am the stained-glass window, the sun glows in my orange body,*
the crack is where I have sinned, you have to do right.

Instead, I chose another sketch called Horse and Rider,
where the rider is the self and the horse is life
and I am the towhee they are riding past. I am preening.
Even then I loved to watch life gallop past me.
Just look at the rider pull back on the reins
when she moves beneath my branch.
Just watch her lay beneath my tree, unmoving.

VII.

When I arrived at the student's house he was shivering,
the cold of the stoop in his bones.
We drove to the city pier. I had a thermos of soup
that burned his tongue, I had a fishing pole but no bait.
We cast the line anyway. Crabs congregated on the stones
beneath our swinging legs, the bay a stained-glass window
in morning's cathedral, sun rays hexing ripples,
sending the seagulls into a hysterics of salt.

The line tugged and I knew we were saved.
But we reeled in a roper-toed boot,
kelp caught in the grommets.
No banished warrior hid inside
waiting to emerge, no lore, no legend.

Who is the fisherman here?
He mimicked, knocking the boot back to the bay.
Red buoys bobbed in the chop.
The day's first ferry berthed in the harbor.

VIII.

The word care has roots in the Gothic kara—
to cry out with, to lament. If it is an act of solidarity
my role was merely to witness his sorrow.
Even that degree of tenderness makes men
uncomfortable. As he slipped into the alley
behind his apartment, parking my car to find a diner,
I thought, *I have been so alone in my pain.*

In each shop the language of the signs changed—
strawberries, fresas, caomei.
Past the stop light, markets gave way to split-levels,
every fifth house abandoned, the lemon trees overflowing,
thriving on neglect, fruit spoiling out of reach.

Outside the Grace Baptist Church a real estate sign
reading Open House for Souls creaked in the breeze.
The vestibule was empty.
It had been years since I'd entered a church
but the nave smelled the same.

I sat in the pews with my sketchbook.
How my hand delighted tracing the bannister's glossy curves,
the ornate crosses scored in the silver candelabra,
gestural line, whisper-wreath of myrrh, the vase of blood
lilies on the altar.

I rendered the lead cames in the windows—
their cross-hatched texture of metallic salt.
A Jacob's ladder streamed through the Last Supper
plaited in crown glass.

I always misrepresent the light—
draw it pouring
when it spills.
Draw it dancing
when stillness brims
inside my chest.

The pastor sat beside me, watching the page fill.
A charcoal arch

> *Not bad...*

above the slatted grate
of the confessional booth,

> *Not bad at all...*

the dark hole
I could never bring myself
to speak through.

Negative Space

IX.

Another death is the death of memory.
But only some memories wither.
It's Darwinian, what remains becomes the standard
against which life is measured—

Grace:

My father's hands
on my sister's corpse,
removing the ring
from her septum,
sliding it on his pinky,
brushing her bleached
bangs into place.

Grief:

Time slowing down.
Time's white sail luffing
against turquoise water.
Time diving from its yacht,
peering through a mask
at pillars of spawning coral.
Time indifferent
to your mourning.

Time do you hear me?
They all say—
just give it time.
Time dropping its anchor,
time in the dinghy.
No matter the size of the waves,
time always
reaches the shore
of its chosen island,
orders a margarita.

x.

The images which form memory are not the ones we expect.
This is what the student remembered of the crash:
On impact a basket of eggs flung from the farmer's lap
in the bus seat beside him. The eggs tossed into the air,
an unborn galaxy released into the aisle—ellipses fixed,
for an instant, an hour?

When he came to he crawled through twisted metal,
past the nun with shards gnawing at her arm,
past the newly dead—
In my dreams their open eyes…azulito—

little blue,
pale blue that hides
in grey,
speckled blue
abandoned in a nest
two days before hatching,
Marian blue
of the virgin's robes—
how she blushes in her portrait
on the tattered card
tucked in his wallet,
blush of vigor, blush
of shame, blush of sky

swilling the sun's blessing
bestowed to all,
even the farmer bled out
on the mountain road
as the engine caught fire,
even his brooding hens,
no one left to feed them.

XI.

The seven deaths need not be chronological.
There are ghosts who have died in body
the seventh death, but retain perfect recollection of their lives.

Unable to create new experiences, their memory sharpens.
These are the ghosts to worry about.
They plant seeds of doubt in certainty, they whisper
in your ear as you sleep, forecasting the next day.

My mother says my father had a ghost like this.
I saw it once sulking in the corner
wearing a frayed, gray blazer,
rolling a cigarette and speaking of a better life,
prodding him to go.

Three Kinds of Shadow

XII.

When I returned from the church, my room was as I left it—
boxes open, my mother watching me from photographs
strewn on the floor, her wrinkles bending toward the years.

Lately she has been resisting the death of the part of the heart
that loves unconditionally.

Only her plants keep it alive, people having failed her.
Transaction is simpler in this kingdom;
water for bloom, pare in November, for fruit come June.

She walks among trained azaleas,
past the monkey flowers,
the passion vine, its oval lobes woven
through the trellis, fiddleheads bursting yellow
song, the swing dance of peas climbing string.

If I die early, if there is agency in reincarnation,
I will come back a snail, I will inch out
into my mother's sorrel and munch the broad greens
with ten thousand teeth.

In the morning, when she puts her fingers
around the whorl of my shell, lowers me into the tin pail,
I will have meant something,
I will have marked my way back to that garden.

XIII.

At dusk, I put on the frayed, gray blazer
and stand in my concrete yard
watching gingko leaves pirouette into winter.

Lives fall away less elegantly.
Each time, like a boot kicked from a pier,
finding home beside the tires full of sludge the snipe eels nest in.

In the middle of the night, the eels emerge, their teeth
glinting in the deep, while up above, my phone glows twice:

Mister they say I can't come back
I have nowhere to go.

I imagine him walking up International—
midnight's patients arriving to their neon convalescence.
Past the sex workers—the cursive *f*s of their painted eyebrows.
Finding the park benches occupied, he walks on,
until he arrives at the church, the only door unlocked.

The nave gaping now, every footstep a transgression
echoing in the aisle, every breath held
as if a ceremony were set to begin.
But no choir rejoices as he enters, no organ groans
in the darkness, no usher greets him with a smile
and a program as he lies down on the pews,

takes the knife from his pocket, guides the blade
through lacquer, carving lines in the grain.

Two lines meeting in opposing directions
give an impression of severity,
or even violence; I read as his class practiced still lifes—

a backlit bowl of eggs beside an empty blue bottle—

If a third line is added,
the opposition is softened
an effect of unity and completeness produced.

XIV.

Awake now, I want to write the student, to comfort him.
But I'm kinder to the dead then I am to the living.
So I write to the farmer, to the ghost
who haunts my father, and to my younger self
who shaved the speedball with a razor,
white rock whittled into three snowy ridges.

I didn't hand my sister the coiled bill,
but I didn't stop her
the last time she said, again.

I crumple the drafts, my hand insists—
again, my sister's name:

> *Dear Rebecca,*
>
> *Whichever words spell out forgiveness*
> *are meant to be sung, not spoken.*
> *If I hum the melody, will you sing along?*

The black ink, dangling, between perforated lines.
A phone wire swings in the night wind,
the waxing moon glances off the bay.

I lean into the shining,
knowing there can be no unity, no completeness,
no finality of vision. Just lines attempting order
and failing, shapes weighted and arranged,
the empty white space holding them apart.

Still, I trace my sister's face on the page.
Her eyes open, gaze settling just beyond me
the way it always did—as if watching a mare
gallop through a crater.

Still, I sing out, maybe she can hear me over the hooves
thudding through the penumbra,
heaving on the pale crust.

CHOSEN LANDSCAPE

Sometimes, the sea plays its green piano
in the 4/4 time of the blues.

Sometimes it plays nocturnes,
the moon knows exactly how to glimmer on.

The way the sea hammers the keys, tonight,
if I could take my sister's hand

I'd lead her into the breaking
waves, so we could become the keys

the sea plays, so we could feel a hundred fingers
strum along our eyes.

And if, when the refrain came, my sister asked,
have I heard this song before?

Would I tell her it's the song our mother sang
as she spread your ashes

on the bluff? The terns riding
slow thermals above us.

Or would I duck beneath the surface,
wrap myself in ringing water

as if it were the worn blanket
she pressed around me

before turning out the lights,
leaving me to dreams of white birds

hunting in gray water.

ACKNOWLEDGMENTS

"Advice for Pallbearers," *upstreet*
"The Hermitage at Laurel Dell," *Harpur Palate*
"Prayer for the Instant City," *Indiana Review*
"Spill," *The Maine Review*
"Looking for Chanterelles in the Oakland Hills," *Poetry East*
"Masa," *RHINO Poetry*
"Rendering the Pose," *Iron Horse Literary Review*
"Chosen Landscape," *Terrain.org*
"I Ask My Sister's Ghost to Take Me with Her," *Harvard Review*
"I Ask My Sister's Ghost to Play a Game of Cribbage," *Southern Indiana Review*

BENJAMIN GUCCIARDI's poems have appeared in *AGNI*, *Best New Poets*, *Indiana Review*, *Orion Magazine*, *Third Coast*, and other journals. He is a winner of *Iron Horse Literary Review*'s 2019 Trifecta Poetry prize, the Milton Kessler Memorial Prize from *Harpur Palate*, and a Dorothy Sargent Rosenberg prize. In addition to writing, he works with refugee and immigrant youth in Oakland, California through Soccer Without Borders, an organization he founded in 2006.

※

COLOPHON

Text is set in a digital version of Jenson, designed by Robert Slimbach in 1996, and based on the work of punchcutter, printer, and publisher Nicolas Jenson. The titles here are in Futura.

❋

NEW MICHIGAN PRESS, based in Tucson, Arizona, prints poetry and prose chapbooks, especially work that transcends traditional genre. Together with *DIAGRAM*, NMP sponsors a yearly chapbook competition.

DIAGRAM, a journal of text, art, and schematic, is published bimonthly at THEDIAGRAM.COM. Periodic print anthologies are available from the New Michigan Press at NEWMICHIGANPRESS.COM.

www.ingramcontent.com/pod-product-compliance
Lightning Source LLC
Chambersburg PA
CBHW031502040426
42444CB00007B/1180